Night Photograph

Lavinia Greenlaw was born [...] lives. After working as an e[...]s, she joined the South Bank C[...] She is now Literature Officer for the London Arts Board. In 1990 she received an Eric Gregory Award.

Lavinia Greenlaw

NIGHT PHOTOGRAPH

faber and faber

LONDON · BOSTON

First published in 1993
by Faber and Faber Limited
3 Queen Square London WC1N 3AU

Phototypeset by Wilmaset Ltd, Wirral
Printed in England by Clays Ltd, St Ives plc

© Lavinia Greenlaw 1993

Lavinia Greenlaw is hereby identified as the author of this
work in accordance with Section 77 of the Copyright, Designs
and Patents Act 1988.

A CIP record for this book is available from the British Library

ISBN 0-571-16894-9

10 9 8 7 6 5 4 3 2 1

for Georgia and Michael

Contents

Acknowledgements

I would like to thank the editors of the magazines and
anthologies in which some of these poems first appeared:
*Critical Quarterly, Iron, New Yorker, The North, Observer,
Poesie Europe, Poetry Review, Stand, TLS* and *The Wide
Skirt; Beneath the Wide Wide Heaven* (eds Sara Dunn and
Alan Scholefield, Virago, 1991), *I Wouldn't Thank You for a
Valentine* (ed. Carol Ann Duffy, Viking Children's Books,
1992), *The Gregory Anthology 1987–1990* (eds Alan
Brownjohn and K. W. Gransden, Hutchinson, 1990),
New Women Poets (ed. Carol Rumens, Bloodaxe, 1990),
Chasing the Sun (Poetry Society/Simon & Schuster, 1992), and
The New Poetry (eds Michael Hulse, David Kennedy and
David Morley, Bloodaxe 1993).

'Boris Goes Fishing' and 'Years Later' were broadcast on
BBC Radio 4.

Some of these poems were published in two pamphlets: *The
Cost of Getting Lost in Space* (Turret Books, 1990) and *Love
from a Foreign City* (Slow Dancer Press, 1992).

I would also like to thank the Society of Authors for the Eric
Gregory Award.

Always remember the moon is a sunlit object.
Expose accordingly.

Monk on a Tractor

The monks on Caldey make perfume and chocolate.
They watch each other grow old
and draft adverts for new recruits.

From April to September, they are surrounded.
The pleasure boat brings holidaymakers
who tidy their faces as they go through the gate,

unprepared for a monk on a tractor
and another hanging underwear on a line.
The sea that swings between the monastery

and my father's house abandons jellyfish,
a used hypodermic, stones and shells that, days later,
give no clue as to why they were picked up.

The wrong wind brings the wrong things home:
raw sewage and, late last summer,
the body of a man who was teaching himself to dive.

Once, a stag swam round the headland.
No one knows where it came from
or who it was that saw it.

Boris Goes Fishing

for Bill Swainson

In my classroom Russia you commented on the weather,
said goodbye to Mother and goodbye to Father,
while I struggled with the tenses
that would let you spend the day by the lake.
Your journey was uneventful. You did not
get lost in a forest, follow strange music
and wander off a path that never saw daylight
to be seduced by a snow queen and rescued by wolves.
I couldn't even send you to Samarkand
to save a princess from being boiled in oil.

You were allowed a blue sky and a friendly dog,
when what you really wanted was a tidal wave
that would empty the Baltic into your basket.
The day passed quietly. You caught three fish
and I managed to get the dog to fall into the water.
At home that evening, Father commented on the weather
while Mother cooked the fish. They could have been
sturgeon travelled north from the Caspian Sea,
pregnant with caviar, flavoured with bison's grass
and served in a blaze of vodka, but I did not

go into detail. Boris, you were a nice boy,
but my hand was more used to carving a desk
than filling a notebook with cramped Cyrillics.
I was fourteen and knew the Russia of storybooks;
I didn't want to make space for the wild grammar,
soft adjectives, accusatives and instrumentals
that would take you there. Instead, you went
to bed at eight o'clock. Mother tucked you up and
commented on the weather. I could not pronounce 'revolution',
so I shut you in a drawer and went dancing.

Sex, Politics and Religion

Her features unfold as she lowers her head
back against the basin. I play for time,
getting the temperature of the water just right.
I have almost grown used to touching old hair
and have learnt to respect a customer's face,
clamping my free hand against the forehead

and forcing the spray tight against the scalp.
I must keep my eyes on my fingers
and must not stare at her feathery cheeks
or the rolling chin that falls away to reveal
her puckered throat and the seamless hole
through which she now has to breathe.

If I understood the words burped into shape
by her new oesophageal voice, I might
ask about cancer and what would happen
if my hand slipped and the harsh foam
dribbled comfortably down a network of gullies,
or if a fly . . . I have to get a look.

The opening is neat and dark,
framed by skin of an unbearable softness.
She has shut her eyes and is smiling
as I massage hard and keep my mind
on the three things I was told by my mother
that a hairdresser should never discuss.

Years Later

I meet my brother in a bar
and he shows me a piece of outer space:
six degrees by six degrees,
a fragment stuffed with galaxies.
He explains how you get pairs of stars
that pull each other into orbit,
for ever unable to touch or part.
When he's gone I remember
you, eighteen and speechless,
and how in the attic of your parents' house
you would take off my clothes,
run a finger as light as a scalpel
across my stomach, then do nothing.
Years later, I wake in the night
still framing the words. And I like
the idea of those stars.

Night Parrot

The feathers were taken from the front wheel of a juggernaut.
All the colours of a winter morning, hinged with pink and bone.
The driver sensed that here was something he had stolen
and had to hide in a box at the back of an empty cupboard
in the attic of an almost empty house. The night parrot.
He had heard some story, a reason not to enter the forest after dark.
And it came true, this curse he couldn't quite remember,
for whatever he now held left him empty-handed,
and he could not sleep for the weight of what it felt like,
the air filled with the impossibility of its cries.

In Such Darkness

The man just buried was your age
so it's hard to know if there's anything to say
as you take your tea and cake outside
away from the kitchen where, all afternoon,
a family has been politely turned over.

Evening brings coolness to an empty room
where you lie down and wait for your wife
to pass by the door and turn on the light
but tonight she finds that the power is gone.
We have lost the comfort of shadows

and surround a table, finding safety in food
and a history of chance and expectation
which says that I will break bone china
and you will keep an old man's silence.
Instead, like the candle between us, you burn:

worn down, intense, repetitious.
No one can stand the meaning of your words
in such darkness. *This is the end . . .*
Thirty years younger, she stamps it out:
I know, I know, any day now . . .

On the doorstep, happy to let it go,
we stand around and watch you fight
with the catch of your umbrella.
It will not release, you push the wrong way,
the handle slips, whatever it is

it takes for ever. It starts to make sense,
that she saturates her voice with calm,
yet will not let you finish a sentence.
I open my mouth but the power is gone.
Someone gets the torches and we each take one.

In the Time of Elizabeth R.

The bishop and his bastard son have been reunited.
Strange faith, Elizabeth, the bread and the blood.
The boy was picked up crossing the city to buy water
on a passport forged by the crippled tailor of Dedham.
The tailor got three days in the village cage.
I saw the bishop kneel in the cathedral, the crowd
fell silent, forgetful of pickpockets and disbelief.
His skin is not good. He will not speak his words
but has them read for him. The church has been swept clean
but incense and mystery persist — a layer of dust
on the sunlit magic of crystals and herbs.
You grow pale at the head of a long walnut dining-table
polished by a serving boy on his knees.
All day, he inches back and forth
in prescribed and supervised motion.
An untouchable finish. No gold knife, no chafing dish,
no loyal finger, leaves a mark.
We bring you affirmation
while new worlds curve the earth beneath your feet
and messages come with the inscrutable fruit
of uncharted lands: *the natives eat them*
with roast wild fowl . . . we must build roads . . . send guns . . .
Look down into that impervious reflection.
There is yet a fixed and perfect heaven.
Traitors' heads? I've got the pictures.

River History

Even then the river carried cargo,
Saxon corn shipped to storehouses on the Rhine.
Taxes were paid in pepper and cloth by the Easterlings,
the German merchants trading from the Steelyard
demolished in the fire of 1666.
Wharves burned like touchpaper, packed
with resin, sulphur, pitch.
The daily catch between London and Deptford
was salmon, eel, smelt and plaice
but the Port Authority preferred to dine
at the Tavern on the best turtle soup in the City
as they argued the height of the wall to be built
against the Mudlarks, Plunderers and Peterboatmen,
intent on their nightly specialized percentage:
cloves from Zanzibar, mother-of-pearl,
tortoiseshell, South American iodine,
West Indian rum, the heavy iron bottles
of Spanish quicksilver, and, from Ivory House,
the occasional mammoth tusk unfrozen in Siberia.
The Empire expanded, cess-pits were banned,
water grew thick with steamships and sewage
and the docks pushed east out into the marshes,
breaking the horizon with a forest of cranes
that unloaded meat, cloth, tobacco and grain
from countries my school atlas still colours pink.
At the Crutched Friars Deposit Office records were kept
of ships in berth, noted daily
by a row of clerks crouched under gaslight
and seven-foot ceilings. Records were kept
of each member of the Union, the fight to be paid

a tanner an hour and not have to climb each day
on another's back and shout to be chosen.
There was always the army.
The Luftwaffe bombed Surrey Commercial Docks
for fifty-seven nights and the timber blazed
for more days than most people kept counting.
Even when every magnetic mine
had been located and cleared, there were dangers.
Centuries of waste had silted the river
till the water ran black over Teddington weir
and a bag of rubbish thrown from London Bridge
took six weeks to ride a dying current
out to the estuary. No swimming, no fish,
and those who fell in had to be sluiced out.
No ships, no work. The industry found itself
caught in the net of passing time,
watching mile after mile of dockland fill
with silence and absence. Land changed hands
in an estate agent's office, short-lease premises
with 'Upstream' and 'Downstream' carved above the doors.
Now the tidal traffic is a slow weekday flow of cars
channeled into streets built before cars were thought of.
They inch round corners, nudge against kerbs,
then settle tight packed against the pavement.
On Butler's Wharf, the only machinery
now in daily use is the tow-away truck:
cruising yellow lines, it pauses to hoist
the solid engineering of a badly parked BMW
into the air with illogical ease.
In Coriander Building, an agency
maintains the plants, the colour scheme is neutral
but the smell of new paint has yet to sink in,
like the spice that still seasons the air after rain.

A film crew arrives, on a costly location shoot
for *Jack the Ripper*. It's a crowded night.
Intent on atmosphere, they've cluttered the alleys
with urchins, trollops and guttersnipes
who drift to the waterfront when they're not working
and gaze across at the biggest, emptiest office block in Europe
and its undefendable, passing light.

From Scattered Blue

for Lesley Davies

I drive back along the river
like I always do, not noticing.
Then something in the light tears open
the smoke from the power-station chimney,

each twist and fold, the construction
of its slow muscular eventual rise
and there, right at the edge of it,
a continual breaking up into sky.

And that's another thing, the sky.
How the mist captures what's left of sunset,
the sodium orange and granite pink
distilled from scattered blue.

The choreography of air-traffic control
and the cranes nested downstream are part of it,
like the bridge and its sugar coat
of broken fairylight. The time of year

when every bird is a brushstroke and the trees
are revealed in a lack of colour. It reminds me
of how we used to talk; how we want sometimes
to do more than just live it.

The Astronomer's Watch

Five months in the desert.
The first rain for centuries.
Local weather fills the telescope lens.

Nothing to do but photograph flowers
that take advantage of these freak conditions
to grow and die. Buried colour –

intense and ancient, unsettled depths
like the red and gold that bloom from a comet
in the heat of passing the sun.

I saw this in a brief transmission
from a space probe, irreparably damaged
by getting too close: the first and last pictures

of the heart of a ball of gas, ice and dust
named after the first two people to sight it
twenty years apart. I sleep whenever

I walk past the bed, feel tired and fall on to it.
The other day I came across my watch.
It surprised me.

The Recital of Lost Cities

It started with the polar ice caps.
A slight increase in temperature and the quiet
was shattered. The Australian Antarctic
wandered all over the Norwegian Dependency
as mountainous fragments lurched free
with a groan like ship's mahogany.

And then there was the continental shift:
everywhere you went, America was coming closer.
Hot weather brought plague and revolution.
Nations disappeared or renamed themselves
as borders moved, in, out, in, out,
with tidal persistence and threat.

Cartographers dealt in picture postcards.
The printing plates for the last atlas
were archived unused. Their irrelevant contours
gathered dust, locked in a vault
to save the public from the past
and the danger of wrong directions.

The sea rose by inches, unravelled the coastline,
eased across the lowlands and licked at the hills
where people gathered to remember names:
Calcutta, Tokyo, San Francisco,
Venice, Amsterdam, Baku,
Alexandria, Santo Domingo . . .

Yosemite

She climbed a tree
and sang to the bears
while he bounced his name
across the valley.

He could make no sense
of the lunatic peaks
thrown together
in a conflict of geology

and closed his eyes
until it was evening
and shadows unfolded
a transient symmetry

that gave him comfort.
Then it grew dark
and she started humming
the one about a picnic.

Spaghetti Western

Eight months' dust and no electrics.
I rehydrate the lizard in the sink,
angle it into a sieve and out of sight.
After dark, we enthuse about candles;
milk curdles in the warmth of the fridge.
There are six bars run by two people.
Cool, knowing, they circle on mopeds
and get there before us, perfectly timed.
We use the phrasebook like a dirty handkerchief
and spill coins, inscrutable treasure.

Shops open when we fall asleep.
The square is always shuttered and barred,
no clues given by casual bystanders
loitering with arms full of wine and bread.
For days you lie in wait with the rubbish
for the boy who drives a dumper truck backwards
down the street at a different time each afternoon.
You never catch him. Nor do you ever
satisfy that thirst for chilled white manzanilla
sipped while playing croquet on an English lawn.

By Sunday you have put together
enough of the language and local connections
to leave a message with the builder's wife.
He plays with the mains box. We rediscover
cold beer and light. Heat and silence
absorb curiosity, simplify response.
We lie on the roof, tracing the movement
of sun and shadow on mountain terraces;
exploring the erotic possibilities
of peeling an orange or playing chess.

One evening, lost in abandoned olive groves
where paths disappear into rock and gorse,
every house we come to is deserted.
There are no more good jokes about snakes.
Climbing out of a cactus-filled ravine
you claim this is where they shot that famous moment:
black stetson, gold tooth, single bullet.
I am picturing it. Then an English voice,
a man who once played football in my village,
calls down from a hidden garden, offers us a drink.

A Change in the Weather

They drive to the beach at Seatown,
entering a scene that the winter light
has overcast with single shades of grey
and brown — old like an old painting.
The child finds the curled fist of an ammonite
and traces its shape with each plump finger,
curious at something so round and so dead.
The man explains about the failure to adapt;
how the shell gives up its flesh,

each pore filling with grains of sand,
turning to stone. The woman walks on
(there is a way of leaving but staying
in sight). Her child runs to give her this,
the only still thing in a shifting world
where land becomes sea then Seatown beach
where she tries to fit her hand to the curves
and studies the clouds, not knowing their names
but looking for a change in the weather.

Thanksgiving on Ghost Ranch

We had no sage, so I flavoured the bird
with *chimaja*, a desert herb the antelope eat.
It is good with eggs, in soup.

I was interested in the hardening green
of the leaves as I slit the skin and squeezed them
beneath the fat – mineral, opaque.

Roasting a turkey is predictable.
Skin dries, pulls away from the flesh,
tissue condenses to inanimate white.

But there are unexpected chemical reactions:
scorched in the oven, coated with grease,
the scent of the desert herb is trapped and withers

to a putrid stink – the smell of meat
that has found time to rot luxuriously
where bones are clean and bleached before dark.

The guests were on their way from Española.
There was no other food. So we packed up the car,
drove to the Black Place, cleared the snow and slept.

I wanted to paint this landscape
but did not know how until, back in New York,
I filled a cow's skull with calico roses.

The Gift of Life

Dr William Pancoast, Philadelphia 1884

In March I inseminated the wife
of a Quaker merchant who was childless.
Extensive tests had led me to believe
the cause of her infertility lay
in the merchant's limited production of sperm.
His wife was brought to the hospital
for a final examination during which
chloroform was applied to face and mouth.
This led to complete unconsciousness
facilitating the insertion of a speculum
and the dilation of the uterine canal.
My finest student provided the sample,
applied with the aid of a rubber syringe
commonly used for agricultural livestock.
I took the additional precaution
of plugging the cervix with cotton rag.
It is now the day after Christmas.
I heard this morning the merchant has been
blessed with a son. God's will be done.

The Patagonian Nightingale

The colonists have 3 flour mills, 8 threshing-machines,
70 reaping machines, 6 pianos, 3 harps, a brass band
and more than 100 violins . . . Music is much cultivated
and Miss Lloyd-Jones is called the Patagonian Nightingale.
                    The Standard, Buenos Aires, 1889

Her hands play with the map on her apron,
Carmarthen and Cardiff slip through her fingers
as exotic and dangerous as the red dragon
that used to hang above the mantelpiece.
Her son fills the room with Spanish gestures.
She sends him to sleep with stories of Wales,
a country drawn from her parents' memories,
where you did not have to fight the weather
but rain fell like a lace curtain
and sunlight passed, barely noticed.

She remembers her father learning to hunt
like the Indians with a three-ball sling,
and bartering rum for meat and skins.
His newspaper was always twelve weeks old
but he inched his way down the columns for hours
and swore this valley was like all valleys,
only, here, spring came in October.

The summer she married, there were dresses from Europe.
She sang at dances every Saturday night
and fell for a cousin who translated himself
into ApJuan, Welsh son of Spanish John,
looking backwards and forwards in two syllables.
He decided the voice of Mary Lloyd-Jones would be
his to cherish and keep safe at home.

Now she meets the train at the new Bethesda or Bryn Crwm
and sends cheese or butter to be sold in Buenos Aires.
After chapel she sifts flour, picks out weevils
and soaks scarce currants in strong cold tea
to make barabrith because her mother did.

Some days she tests that remote language
and tells anyone who'll listen what they already know:
how her pregnant mother crossed the Atlantic,
three months of hymns and seasickness,
and how Mary was the first Welsh child to be born
in Patagonia. And they named the hills for her.

The Man Whose Smile Made Medical History

On dead afternoons my brother would borrow
rubber gloves and wellington boots
to chance the electrics of the ancient projector.

We would interrupt fifty-year-old summers where
a woman I now know in nappies and a walking frame
played leapfrog on a beach in West Wales

with a man whose smile made medical history.
The First World War revealed the infinite
possibilities of the human form,

so when in '16 he was sent back from France
without his top lip, the army doctors
decided to try and grow him a new one.

They selected the stomach as the ideal place
from which to tease a flap of skin
into a handle that could be stretched

and sewn to what was left of his mouth.
This additional feature was surgically removed
once it had fed the regeneration

of a thankfully familiar shape.
All I can find in my grandfather's face
to record the birth of plastic surgery

is the tight shyness he pulls into a grin,
unaware that scientific progress
which had saved his reflection could do nothing

to save his life. A doctor, aged thirty-four,
he died of viral pneumonia,
having recently heard of antibiotics.

In the Zoo after Dark

No full moon or forest fire.
Unnatural light
takes shape and stays there.
Shadows adjust
to what could be night.

Animals intended
to live an ocean apart
have got an idea of each other.
All day
the lion has watched
a dolphin curve into vision
with the promise of its element,
the taste of salt.

There is containment
and release:
the instinct of the death-watch beetle
to beat its head against the wall
in love song,

or the stillness of the golden eagle,
wings folded, waiting
for the sky to break.

Electricity

The night you called to tell me
that the unevenness between the days
is as simple as meeting or not meeting,
I was thinking about electricity —
how at no point on a circuit
can power diminish or accumulate,
how you also need a lack of balance
for energy to be released. *Trust it*.
Once, being held like that,
no edge, no end and no beginning,
I could not tell our actions apart:
if it was you who lifted my head to the light,
if it was I who said how much I wanted
to look at your face. *Your beautiful face*.

Linear, Parallel, Constant

Driving down to Jericho
my car was overtaken
by a trio of missiles.
This was a precise migration –
linear, parallel, constant.
An exact miracle
on a straight road
over flat land
under clear sky.
Such mathematical beauty
filled me with the same
superstition and certainty
that send a rocket
to meet the heavens
carrying the name of a Roman god.

Galileo's Wife

He can bring down stars.
They are paper in my hands
and the night is dark.

He knows why stone falls and smoke rises,
why the sand on the shore in the morning
is gone in the afternoon.

He gobbles larks' tongues from Tuscany
and honey from Crete. If only he could
measure me and find my secrets.

*

I have dropped pebbles into water
six hundred times this morning.
The average speed of descent

was three pulsebeats with a half-beat variable,
allowing for the different angle and force
with which each pebble hit the water.

Galileo wants me to explain my results.
He lectures on naval engineering
at the university tonight.

*

There has been a fire.
Our children were trapped in a tower.
He watched them fall, a feather, a stone,

and land together. He dictated notes
and ordered their bodies weighed before burial.
I sleep among their clothes.

I must leave Pisa.
He says I am to locate the edge of the world.
Galileo must complete the map.

He has a pair of velvet slippers.
It takes half an hour to lace my boots.
I like to keep my feet on the ground.

*

There is a cloud over Dalmatia.
It is the colour of my wedding dress.
Shadows burn stone.

The bears in Natolia
follow me to the marketplace
and carry food to the houses of the poor.

In Persia I walk east all day
across a desert. I look back at sunset.
The desert is a sea of orchids.

Tartaria is cold. Horses dance
on the path down the ravine. I fall
and the frozen air catches me.

In China I come to a walled city
where they know how to make a powder
that turns the sky to thunder and gold.

In the land of paper houses, a tidal wave
carries me up into the mountains.
I feed children with the fish in my pockets.

I fall asleep beside the ocean
and wake up in the New World
where my footsteps split yellow rock wide open.

A wind I refuse to name carries me home.
Galileo opens the door. I draw a circle
and he closes my eye with a single blow.

*

He says my boots have kept him awake
for the fifteen years I've been away.
He gives me pebbles and water.

Every night he is at the university
proving the existence of the edge of the world.
His students sleep and applaud.

I leave the truth among his papers
and thank the bears of Natolia
that I never taught him how to write.

Beyond Gravity

What was it
that scorched your face
and stole your sleep?

An eagle's feather
or the hand of someone
lost to you?

Terror. Desire.
All that is left
of the absolute disintegration

beyond gravity.

Like sun on water,
a ripple of gold
at the corner of the eye

as heavy skirts
fold into the river,
wings close.

Thirty Miles North-West

There were thirty miles he never travelled,
north-west to the sea which was all he talked of:
the breakable blue of a northern summer,
thin as a bird's egg, soft as a blanket,
the light of a ferry-crossing out of Danzig,
endless cement and tarpaulin scattered
with the quartz of a Baltic winter afternoon.

He tasted the air and predicted its colour —
lambswool, pigeon feather, oil, steel —
and believed he'd never lose his way
among the deadly architecture of its sudden cities.
He heard its music in shattering glass,
dropped cutlery, a river of grain,
sheets thrown into the air above a bed.

He felt it on his lips in samphire and dulse,
and caught its scent through an open window
the morning after five days' rain.
And in his pulse, the percussion of its breaking,
the pendulum swing of its tides. Thirty miles
he never travelled — towards the possibility
that there might be no words for it.

The Cost of Getting Lost in Space

I

On New Year's Eve, the keeper of the clock
balanced time with the help of old money.
His threepenny bits outwitted the earth
which flexed in its orbit again and again
to create an extra second among the strokes
of midnight. Each person raised a glass
and counted from one to twelve
while the keeper wove a little into every chime,
adding the possibility of a word, a gesture,
a brief incandescence that could have made
a different future, or no difference at all.
It was there. Nobody noticed, but it was there.

II

From a distance of ninety-three million miles,
a solar flare unravelled the earth's
magnetic field and set a cat among
a thousand pigeons racing from France.
Prized for flying straight home they flew
straight along lines that no longer met.
The sky shrugged off its known geography
and spun those birds beyond direction.
They helter-skeltered down on to the Scilly Isles,
sent nervous owners running to the map,
but it might as well have been Outer Mongolia –
the finish was in Newcastle, nobody won.

III

A phone call after the pub had shut.
If you free yourself of the human scale,
there is only futility. If it is
futility, you cannot be free
of the human scale. Like the answer
you gave me once in a dream:
I can't see anything in this mist.
Then open your eyes! A burst of peace.
You raced home to write till morning.
The computer belonged to someone else.
At five a.m., you pressed the wrong button.
Nobody had stopped to take notes.

Moby Dick Suite

The pianist finds a phone box by the station
and asks his wife what he is doing in Wolverhampton.
She is tired of giving directions but he cannot read maps
so she tells him to get a taxi to the concert hall
and after the performance to go straight to the hotel.
He has been lost for ten years, since the day
he looked into the mirror, saw the madness of his father,
and started to hunt him with music.

The pianist always said yes to everything
and let his wife talk herself out of all dignity.
He was confused by how she made a room safe
but filled it with a bad smell and locked the windows.
Pursued by the cruel voice of a dead friend
he turned, not to garlic or a rabbit's foot,
but to cutting crosses in his forehead
seen in his reflection as a saving grace.

Tonight, he will surprise the audience
with his fat fingers and flat voice.
He will play the final scene where Captain Ahab
falls from the boat to the back of the whale and drowns,
lashed down by the rope of his own harpoon.
The audience will hear him out, relieved
when there is nothing left but still waters
and the prettiness of seagulls overhead.

These days the pianist cannot have bad dreams:
the disconnection of electric shock
has safely straightened every mirror.
He wraps up warm, watches old films,
and sends someone else after his monster.
On screen, the Captain keeps his distance
and never fails to meet the kind of death
that the pianist himself had always wanted.

Anchorage

The fish factory wriggles free of the Baltic
and takes a firm grip on the North Sea.
Echo and sonar are its web, so fine
it can snare a single cod at a thousand feet.

Trawler crews used to taste the air,
then lower a lead weight coated with grease
thick enough to bring back the sea bed;
rock, shell or sand was all they wanted.

Grey steel on grey water under grey sky
moving west with the weather map:
Viking, Fair Isle, Hebrides, Malin,
murky republics bound by salt and oil

carry the Russian sailor to meet dry land
where two years and seven hundred miles
have brought me to your wedding.
The streets are too wide, the houses too small

and I'm scared of getting my face wet.
We run into each other's arms,
our hands reveal a brother and sister
of rock, shell, sand. I am close enough

to see the tear form and melt in your eye.
Inch by inch, the Russian sailor
studies the horizon. It never falters.
The ground stays still beneath his feet,

he needs a drink. The cargo is packed
in eighty-pound blocks of suspended animation:
huge, beautiful fish taken from the nets
and returned to water but not enough water.

*

I get tired of whale song and head south
away from five-hour nights and a blazing moon
that tricks me into thinking up mysteries.
Close to the Arctic, nets cast up
uncertain shapes. The North Pole wavers.

Those seven hundred miles are back in place
but confetti falls from me with every step.
I cannot get if off my hands,
this mess of salty, almost silver scales
leeched in a moment of helpless intimacy,
these leftover scraps of faded tissue
once strong enough to carry the ocean.

Behind the Light

He is happy off the land, out there with his boy,
away from the weight of a lifetime of singing
the mountains to sleep. Out there his boat
rolls through peaks like a tongue through butter.

The boy has grown up without streetlight.
He is drawn to the mackerels' fractured glitter
as they flare beneath the surface, flop into the boat.
His father, too, is blinded by the shining:
last year, dazzled by the hundred fish
that had queued for his hook, he misread the elements
and fell from a dry shade of blue into a deep one.

The sea inched its way into his blood,
then flicked him on to the rocks to be found
by a girl whose brother had drowned here the year before;
a girl who sucked the sea from his lungs,
spat out this stranger's vomit and saliva,
and hammered at the broken machinery of his chest
for the two hours it took the ambulance to come.

Yet tonight he feels so safe out there,
wrapped in the blanket of a summer night sky,
his memory washed clean by the sea.
Later, at the house, he rinses the fish.
He has no need of them and they have no need of water.
The boy is in bed, framing the moment coming home
when he caught the blast of a cat's eyes with his torch.

She cannot sleep and goes out by the back door,
up on to the mountain, away from a husband
who still refuses to learn how to swim.
She climbs to a place where nothing moves,
nothing confuses or catches her eye;
where she can lie down and bury her face
in what little earth the ice age has left her.

Estuary

air carries the taste
of ocean-going liners

shadows of Canada geese
colour the salt grass

water trickles inland
suggests the threat of nesting swans

black Essex mud
refuses to take shape

I can live with this promise

that nothing is in place
but everything is here

Closer

Your touch surprises me
like a breath of sea air in the city
and I don't know which way to move
in the opposing landscapes of my senses.
As if, crossing a street I have lived in for years,

the taste of salt comes to my mouth
and I lose sight of what I'm walking towards:
a window that has caught and reflected
all that is familiar; or the edge of this island
from where I can at last look out.

Love from a Foreign City

Dearest, the cockroaches are having babies.
One fell from the ceiling into my gin
with no ill effects. Mother has been.
I showed her the bite marks on the cot
and she gave me the name of her rat-catcher.
He was so impressed by the hole in her u-bend,
he took it home for his personal museum.
I cannot sleep. They are digging up children
on Hackney Marshes. The papers say
when that girl tried to scream for help,
the man cut her tongue out. Not far from here.
There have been more firebombs,
but only at dawn and out in the suburbs.
And a mortar attack. We heard it from the flat,
a thud like someone dropping a table.
They say the pond life coming out of the taps
is completely harmless. A law has been passed
on dangerous dogs: muzzles, tattoos, castration.
When the labrador over the road jumped up
to say hello to Billie, he wet himself.
The shops in North End Road are all closing.
You can't get your shoes mended anywhere.
The one-way system keeps changing direction,
I get lost a hundred yards from home.
There are parts of the new *A to Z* marked simply
'under development'. Even street names
have been demolished. There is typhoid in Finchley.
Mother has brought me a lavender tree.

A Letter from Marie Curie

The girl dying in New Jersey
barely glances at the foreign words
but she likes the stamp.
It is a kind of pale blue
she hasn't seen much of.
The lawyer who brought the letter
talks of a famous scientist
who found the magic ingredient
that made the clockfaces she painted
shine in the dark. He doesn't say
that each lick of the brush
took a little more radium
into her bones, that in
sixteen hundred years
if anything remained of her
it would still be half as radioactive
as the girl is now,
thumbing through the atlas
she asked her sister to borrow.
He explains that Marie Curie
is anaemic too, but the girl
isn't listening. She's found France;
it's not so big. The lawyer shrugs:
She says to eat plenty of raw calves' liver.

The Innocence of Radium

With a head full of Swiss clockmakers,
she took a job at a New Jersey factory
painting luminous numbers, copying the style
believed to be found in the candlelit backrooms
of snowbound alpine villages.

Holding each clockface to the light,
she would catch a glimpse of the chemist
as he measured and checked. He was old enough,
had a kind face and a foreign name
she never dared to pronounce: Sochocky.

For a joke she painted her teeth and nails,
jumped out on the other girls walking home.
In bed that night she laughed out loud
and stroked herself with ten green fingertips.
Unable to sleep, the chemist traced each number

on the face he had stolen from the factory floor.
He liked the curve of her eights;
the way she raised the wet brush to her lips
and, with a delicate purse of her mouth,
smoothed the bristle to a perfect tip.

Over the years he watched her grow dull.
The doctors gave up, removed half her jaw,
and blamed syphilis when her thighbone snapped
as she struggled up a flight of steps.
Diagnosing infidelity, the chemist pronounced

the innocence of radium, a kind of radiance
that could not be held by the body of a woman,
only caught between her teeth. He was proud
of his paint and made public speeches
on how it could be used by artists to convey

the quality of moonlight. Sochocky displayed
these shining landscapes on his walls;
his faith sustained alone in a room
full of warm skies that broke up the dark
and drained his blood of its colour.

His dangerous bones could not keep their secret.
Laid out for X-ray, before a single button was pressed,
they exposed the plate and pictured themselves
as a ghost, not a skeleton, a photograph
he was unable to stop being developed and fixed.

Science for Poets

We drive to your laboratory
on a Sunday morning. Those incubated cells
are about to divide, and you must feed them.

Behind the hospital's airport welcome
of franchised chocolates, soft toys and flowers,
I'm surprised by the room. Sure, there are

bottles on shelves
and enough radioactive-warning stickers to keep me
standing very still, but the air

is civil service
and the furniture, an indigestible brown.
You open the door of an ordinary fridge,

pull on rubber gloves, select a jar
and dose a plastic tray of dots
with the swift repetition of the conveyor belt.

I want bunsen burners;
the surprise weight of a bottle of mercury,
its threat of death by cracked thermometer.

I want a scalpel, a bull's eye,
its slit cornea and slippery lens, the grubby innards
of an earthworm pinned out on a board;

to catch sight of physics
in the force of a stiletto heel on a dance hall's
wooden floor; to discuss the uses

of labelled jars —
acetone for the removal of nail polish,
sulphuric acid for the serial killer.

I miss the Monday afternoons
of inactivity under the microscope, the Petri dish
and pH scale with its odd capital letter.

Now, I watch you
measuring deep into decimal places to record
each molecular shift, in search of an answer

or an answer that fits,
or else in hope of some wild enlightenment
that without your eye for detail, I'd surely miss.

In the Picture Palace

for Patrick Yarker

I was in Leeds, you were in Southend,
but we were on the same corner:
dog shit, pot holes, no streetlight.
On either side shop fronts,
bill posters and broken glass
where there used to be a locksmith,
a butcher and a woman who sold
a hundred different kinds of gloves.
The only cinema in town
to never make it as a bingo hall.
Original features are there somewhere
behind brushed nylon, red flock wallpaper
and twenty coats of corporation paint.
The carpet is original. It sticks to your shoes.
You must buy sweets and they are all noisy:
chocolates that roll down the aisle like cannonballs,
explosions of caramel;
you miss the punchline and break your teeth.
After the adverts for a local restaurant
and a secondhand garage that's just closed down,
and the trailers for excitement forthcoming
at a cinema near you soon but not this one,
you settle down, open to new ideas
about sex, violence and the car chase.
It ends just after the last bus has gone.
You walk through the foyer and the staff line up
by the door to thank all five of you
for coming here tonight. *Safe journey home.*

You smile too hard and take a programme
like a promise but out on the street
it doesn't take long to forget how it ended.
Without wanting to you move away from the story,
back to a familiar part of town
where there are road signs you don't need anymore.

For the First Dog in Space

You're being sent up in Sputnik 2,
a kind of octopus with rigor mortis.
Ground control have sworn allegiance
to gravity and the laws of motion;
they sleep without dreams,
safe in the knowledge
that a Russian mongrel bitch
can be blasted through the exosphere
at seven miles a second,
but can never stray far from home.
You will have no companion,
no buttons to press, just six days' air.
Laika, do not let yourself be fooled
by the absolute stillness
that comes only with not knowing
how fast you are going. As you fall
in orbit around the earth, remember
your language. Listen to star dust.
Trust your fear.

Suspension

Two hundred and forty-five feet above the mud,
I play with the story of the bridge's construction.
How Brunel, in his early twenties,
was a half-drowned invalid hiding in Bristol,
looking for a way to win back faith
after the collapse of his tunnel under the Thames.

I curl over the railings, unable to grasp
the push-and-pull dynamics of Brunel's success,
a puzzle for my building-brick perceptions.
He used secondhand chains to hold up a seven-
hundred-foot span. He was a sick man.
It is safer to look away from the light

and test the vertigo that comforts those
who come here to die. It is a popular spot
and the road below has to be protected
by a shelf described as a 'body stop'.
I stay on the bridge, laugh at its ghosts,
make jokes about accident and suicide;

then I start to accept Brunel's equation,
the simplicity holding it all in place.
Now it looks too easy, I can't go on,
my sense of balance is suddenly lost
along with my ignorance, the framework of
the physics of what keeps us from falling.

Night Photograph

Crossing the Channel at midnight in winter,
coastline develops as distance grows,
then simplifies to shadow, under-exposed.

Points of light – quayside, harbour wall,
the edge of the city –
sink as the surface of the night fills in.

Beyond the boat, the only interruption
is the choppy grey-white we leave behind us,
gone almost before it is gone from sight.

What cannot be pictured is the depth
with which the water moves against itself,
in such abstraction the eye can find

no break, direction or point of focus.
Clearer, and more possible than this,
is the circular horizon.

Sea and sky meet in suspension,
gradual familiar textures of black:
eel-skin, marble, smoke, oil –

made separate and apparent by the light
that pours from the sun on to the moon,
the constant white on which these unfixable

layers of darkness thicken and fade.
We are close to land, filtering through
shipping lanes and marker buoys

towards port and its addition of colour.
There is a slight realignment of the planets.
Day breaks at no particular moment.